MONEY
RULES

MONEY RULES

The Simple Path to Lifelong Security

JEAN CHATZKY

RODALE

Rodale books may be purchased for business or promotional use or for special sales. For information, please write to:
Special Markets Department, Rodale, Inc., 733 Third Avenue, New York, NY 10017

Printed in the United States of America
Rodale Inc. makes every effort to use acid-free ♾, recycled paper ♺.

Book design by Mark Michaelson with George Karabotsos

Front cover photography by Thomas MacDonald/Rodale Images
Back cover photography by Dave Moser

Library of Congress Cataloging-in-Publication Data

Chatzky, Jean Sherman.
    Money rules : the simple path to lifelong security / Jean Chatzky.
        p.   cm.
    ISBN 978–1–60961–860–5   paperback
    1. Finance, Personal.   2. Investments.   3. Retirement income—Planning.
I. Title.
HG179.C53583   2012
332.024'01—dc23   2012000177

Distributed to the trade by Macmillan

2   4   6   8   10   9   7   5   3   1   paperback

We inspire and enable people to improve their lives and the world around them.

www.rodalebooks.com

For my parents, who taught me the rules,
my husband, who helps me keep them,
and my kids, who I hope will (someday)
know them by heart.

Contents

Introduction

You worry about your money. Most people do. You're concerned that there isn't enough of it for today—and even more concerned that there won't be enough to get you through tomorrow. Statistics show that 50 percent of people will run out of money in retirement. That's half of the retired population. That's terrifying.

And that won't be you.

Why not? It's very simple: If you follow the rules in this book, you will have a lifetime of financial security and eliminate most, if not all money stress.

I know this because I've spent the past quarter century knee-deep in the world of people and their money. I've watched how we make it, save it, spend it, borrow it, invest it, and protect it. And I can tell you that there aren't that many things separating the people who succeed financially from those who blow it.

The folks who succeed do a few elemental things over and over. They adhere to a concrete and simple set of Money Rules. Because they do, their financial futures are not in jeopardy. They don't have to worry about having enough cash to pay their bills, save for tomorrow, and take care of their families—because they will. They don't have to worry about running out of money in retirement—because they won't.

You can be one of these people.

To understand what's been holding you back, simply answer the following question: How would you describe your relationship with money?

I asked a random sample of Americans that question and here's what they said: Confusing. Frightening. Criminal. Chaotic. Stressful. Unstable. Precarious. Necessary evil. Unnecessarily complex.

Those negative feelings present a big problem. When you're frightened of something, the human tendency is to retreat rather than tackle. And retreating from your finances is something you can't afford to do.

You are much more responsible for your own finances than previous generations. They had pensions provided by corporations and managed by pros. You have a 401(k) to manage yourself. They had health insurance that came—*gratis*—with their jobs. You are being asked to contribute more for that coverage every year. They had confidence that Social Security and Medicare would last as long as they did. Many of us (maybe even most of us) do not.

Over the years, I have been told that the thing I'm best at is taking complicated financial subjects and putting them in words the average Joe or Jane can understand. I think I can do this because I am that average Jane. I'm not an economist or a financial advisor or a CPA. I'm a journalist—as well as a consumer, small-business owner, employee, client, taxpayer, homeowner, wife, ex-wife, mother, daughter, sister, and friend. Whenever I tackle a new investment or insurance policy or piece of tax code, I am aiming to understand it well enough to make use of it in my own life. And once I've done that, I can help you understand it, too.

Getting to the bottom of these things has become a part of my DNA. That's why when the president announces that he's got a new program to help students deal with their overwhelming student loan debts, or massive numbers of people want to leave their banks after the addition of a new layer of fees, you'll often find me on TV teaching you—step by step—how to deal. The problem is that between the speed at which we're living and the frequency with which these financial changes (changes in laws, changes in fees, changes in everything) are coming at us, sometimes things fall through the cracks.

We need simplicity. A means of looking at most of the money decisions we're asked to make and being able to say: Yes. Or no.

That simplicity is possible.

Over my career, I've come up with a set of Money Rules that I follow (and tell others to follow) religiously. And I'm not the only one. Financial advisers, analysts, bankers, accountants, lawyers, as well as plenty of smart people in nonfinancial professions have their own Money Rules.

This book pulls them together. First, I made my own list. Then I collected from others. Then I vetted both. I got rid of the ones that didn't make sense and the ones that didn't hold water. I got rid of the ones that just didn't feel right. In fact, I got rid of more rules than I held onto. You'll see the ones that passed all of my tests on the pages that follow.

Some rules are self-explanatory. For those that aren't, I've included the logic. It's important to understand why these rules are rules. You will be better off if you never pull money out of your 401(k) before you retire, just as you will be better off if you never shop angry. Those are facts. But if you understand why, you're more likely not just to commit the rules to memory but also to stick by them because they make so much sense.

But before you read on, there are two guiding principles I want you to think about. These will color what you take away from the rules in the sections that follow.

Principle #1:
Personal finance is more personal than it is finance.

You have to make the decisions that are right for you—not right for your best friends or your siblings or even your mother—but right for you and for your family. That may mean leaving cash in the bank because it enables you to sleep at night while the "experts" are telling you to invest that money so it can grow. It may mean taking a lower paying job because you think you'll actually enjoy the work. It may mean deciding you'll work a few extra years because you can't stand the thought of loading up your kids with student loans. Whatever personal choices you make, make them thoughtfully and with a plan to get you from here to there. That's key, because along the way, I guarantee there will be stops and starts. There will be emergencies and surprises. And there will be people (sometimes people who love you) who think you're doing it all wrong. That's because. . . .

Principle #2:
Money is simple—people make it complicated.

A person's behavior around money is emotional, sometimes nonsensical, often frustrating and maddening. Here's proof: If I were to take any other resource—whether it's a basic one like water or a luxury like a bottle of champagne—and say I'm going to divvy it up among you and a dozen of your colleagues, there would be a feeling that it should be split fairly. But if I say I have some extra money, there's more infighting involved. People start to ask, who's more or less worthy? Who's more or less needy? It becomes a value judgment. There's morality associated with it. And, therefore, it's much more complicated. Try to keep this in mind as you make financial decisions for yourself—and weigh in on the decisions of others.

So, let's get to it, remembering that these rules are brief on purpose. They are made to remove complexity and embrace simplicity. They're also easy to remember because if you can remember them, then you can follow them. And that is precisely the point.

PART 1

Make Money

The money that goes out—whether you spend it, save it, invest it, or give it away—has to come from somewhere.

That generally means earning it.

And that's a good thing.

Getting paid is an indication that others value what you do, how you think, and who you are.

All of those things are a boost to your self-esteem.

The rules in this section will help you understand how to earn what you're worth, how to extract the most happiness possible from those earnings, and when, in fact, you shouldn't do that particular work but instead delegate it to someone else.

1.
Your job is your most important investment.

For years, you were told your home and retirement accounts were your greatest assets. Wrong. If the Great Recession has proven anything, it's that your job—more specifically, your earning power—is by far your greatest asset. Protect your financial security by treating this asset like any other investment. If your work profile is risky, you're paid on commission or bonuses rather than straight salary, or your job security is largely tied to the economy, it's like a stock. If it's more stable, you work for the government, you're one of the lucky few who still has a traditional pension plan, or you're a tenured teacher or college professor—you're essentially holding a bond. Consider this when you fashion your asset allocation: Those in "stock-like" jobs need to account for that by being a little less aggressive in their other investments. Those with job security can take a little more risk.

2.
Your education is your second-most important investment.

The rising cost of college has led to a populist cry that college degrees aren't worth the money. That's completely backward. A study from Georgetown University shows the value of a college degree is going up. The typical worker with less than a high school diploma will earn $973,000 over the course of a career. The typical professional (think doctor or lawyer) will earn $3.6 million. College grads fall halfway between. The pay gap between those who go to college and don't has gotten wider—and is expected to continue to grow. This isn't just an income gap—it's also a "social" one. College grads are more likely to get and stay married, to have strong networks of friends, to be active in their communities, and are less likely to be obese and smoke (both are wealth reducers—see rules #82 and #83). It's also important to note that graduating from college is more important than where you graduate from college (although a 4-year degree does pay off better than a 2-year one does). Bottom line: The more you learn, the more you expand your horizons and rack up cold, practical experience, the more you're worth to someone who needs your talents. Your stock can rise in any economy.

3.
Know your worth on the open market.

Are you worth more than you're earning today? Or less? If you don't know, that is a huge problem. If you're under-earning, you're losing money every day you're not asking for more. If you're overpaid, you're ripe for the chopping block, and you'd better update your skills or improve your productivity. You can find salary information online. Better yet, ask a friend or colleague at a competing firm, "What would someone with my skills be paid at your company?"

4.
If you don't ask for more money, the answer will always be "no."

Here's a shocker: In 2011, newly-trained female doctors earned salaries that averaged $17,000 less than newly-trained male doctors. It's not that women were picking less-lucrative specialties or that they were asking for more flexible work schedules. That used to be the case, but not this time. The difference this time was a problem that's existed for years. Women don't ask. Whether you're a woman or a man, you have to ask for the money you want. The answer may not be the one you're looking for. But if you don't ask, the answer will always be "no."

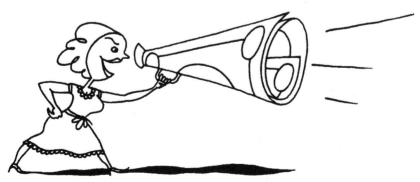

5.

You're never more valuable than when someone else wants you.

If you've been at your job more than a few years, chances are you're underpaid. The last few years have been some of the leanest for salary increases in three decades. Who did receive a decent raise? The guy or gal who jumped ship, that's who. Someone else recognized that person's value. You can do the same, but note: This gambit works best if your last performance evaluation was stellar and if taking the new job is something you're actually willing to do. That's the best way on the planet to earn a raise.

6.
The four most powerful words in any negotiation: "Can you do better"?

You're sitting in the office of the person who's dying to be your new boss. He's just offered you a job that you really want with the title you've been craving. The only hitch: The salary isn't where you'd hoped it would be. Don't commit—at least not until you ask, "Can you do better"? It's the perfect haggle. You sound as if you know there's wiggle room, and you're willing to let him work his magic. And note: This works just as well when you're on the phone with the cable company, at the mechanic for an oil change, talking to a mortgage rep about locking in a "refi" rate.
It even—I know from experience—works with teenage kids.

7.
"More money" won't always make you "more happy."

The next time you're considering taking a job "just for the money" remember this: Money only buys happiness to a point. Beyond that, more money makes no difference in how happy you feel. According to some Nobel laureates, $75,000 buys happiness. That's an average that varies regionally—happiness is more expensive in Manhattan, NY, than in Manhattan, Kansas. But the message is this: As long as you earn enough to pay your mortgage or rent, put gas in a car that's not a clunker, eat what you want when you want to, and take the occasional vacation and, oh yes, save a decent chunk of whatever you're bringing in, more money will not make you more happy. Coming up short on any of those basic wants and needs, however, will make you miserable.

8.
The more time you spend looking, the less happy you'll be with what you find.

When an opportunity seems good enough, take it. Researchers surveyed job-hunting college seniors and found that those who searched for perfection generally did land jobs paying 20 percent more. Unfortunately, those former students liked those jobs much less. That makes sense. If you're looking for the ultimate opportunity, the one you eventually choose is destined to fall short. The not-so-picky students were happier with their jobs. The same applies to any big purchase. Spend days searching for the best flat-screen TV and you'll always doubt your choice. Find one in a few hours that fits all your needs at a decent price? You're gonna love it.

9.

An hour of your time is worth _____.

Here's a quick and dirty way to compute your hourly rate. Remove the last three zeros from your annual salary and divide the remaining number in half. For example, if you earn $30,000 a year, that gives you a rate of $15 an hour. If you make $100,000, it's $50 an hour. Use this handy formula—in combination with your enjoyment/hatred of the task at hand—to decide when it's okay to hire others and which tasks aren't worth doing at all. The weeding of the garden you could hire someone to do for $15 an hour? If you hate it and earn more, hire help. If you love it and earn more, don't. And if you earn less yourself, plug in your iPod, pour yourself a cold one, and start digging.

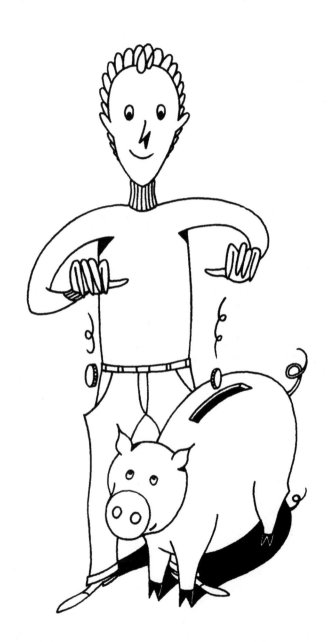

PART 2

Save Money

Saving money is not the easiest thing to do. It requires you to prioritize your needs and wants tomorrow ahead of your needs and wants today.

Human beings aren't wired to be good at that.

And that is unfortunate because the safety nets provided by the government and employers in the past are looking pretty shaky these days.

The result: Saving money for your own future has never been more important.

The rules in this section make it simple and painless to sock away money.

10.
Live below your means. Period.

When I hear people suggest that you "live on what you make," I always shake my head. If you're living on what you make, you're spending every dime. The key is to live on less than you make. This is non-negotiable. Why? Because if you do it consistently, you're automatically saving consistently. Aim to save at least 10 percent of what you earn—15 percent if you're more than age 35 and haven't started yet. If you can't hit 10 percent, start by saving something. If you can do 3 percent, start at 3. If you can do 5 percent, start at 5. And if you can save more than 15, by all means do that, too. Then—with the same enthusiasm you brought to watching your lima bean plant take root in grade school—watch that stash start to grow. Take pride in it. You're accomplishing something very few people can. And that will inspire you to set aside more.

11.

If you can't see it and you can't touch it, you won't spend it.

This is why saving in a 401(k) plan works. The money is swiped out of your pay before it ever lands in your checking account so you never see it. It's invisible, which makes it safe, for out-of-sight means you can't pull it out of the ATM. There are also painful barriers to getting the money out. If you did want to spend your 401(k) stash before age $59\frac{1}{2}$, you'd have pay income taxes that can eat up 20 to 30 percent of your total, plus a 10 percent penalty. That hurts.

Don't stop at a 401(k). Have money swiped out of your checking account as soon as you get paid. Barricade it by parking it in places that penalize you for early withdrawal like 529 college savings accounts, IRAs, and certificates of deposit. Even putting the money in an Internet savings account that doesn't come with an ATM card can do the trick surprisingly well.

12.
Save more with every raise.

Here's what happened the last time you got a raise: You celebrated by taking the family out to dinner, splurged on that new coat you'd been eyeing, and started planning a vacation. Here's what happened to your net worth: Nada. If your spending rises with your salary, you're always going to be behind in the savings game. Make this a rule: Every increase in pay comes with a commensurate increase in how much you're socking away. In other words, the first call you make isn't to your spouse to share the good news; it's to the benefits department to ask them to increase your 401(k) contribution.

13.
There's no such thing as chump change.

$100 is not a lot of money. Save it every week, however, and invest it in a retirement account where you earn a conservative 6 percent, and keep doing it for 30 years and you'll have $435,557. In 40 years, you'll have more than twice that. And that is a lot of money.

14.

Financial plans don't fail people. People fail to plan.

The only way to find financial security is to draw yourself a map. Folks who have specific financial plans that detail what they want—say, retirement at 67 with a paid-off mortgage, membership at the local golf club, and enough money to take two trips to the Caribbean a year—save more than people who don't have specific financial plans. Why? Because human beings are easily distracted (especially by shiny things). So unless you have a road map that tells you where you're going, it is very, very hard to get there. It's not that the map will never change. One day you'll wake your significant other up with a rousing shake and tell her (or him): "I don't want to retire in this house. I want to move to Belize!" At which point you can make a new road map and follow that until, inevitably, you change your mind again. Revising your specific plans for the future is far better than not having any plans at all.

15.
Emergencies happen.

Your car will break down or the roof will spring a
leak or one of another thousand things will go wrong.
And you need to have money for when they do.

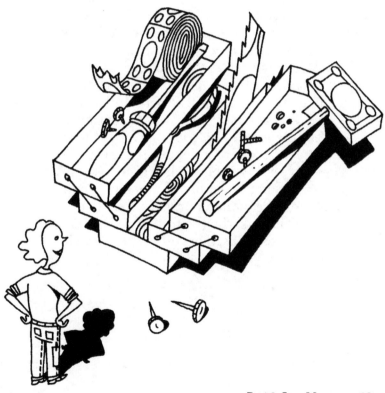

16.
The best way to be comfortable is to be slightly uncomfortable.

Putting that aforementioned money aside for emergencies will be easier if you're not feeling too satisfied with your lot in life. Researchers asked a group of people to rate their happiness on a scale of 1 to 10, where 1 is misery and 10 is bliss. Know what? The 8s have it over the rest. That's because 8s, while happy, are not so blissed-out that they believe everything in the future will be beautiful and rosy. They believe that emergencies do happen and as a result they plan for them. They buy life insurance (when they have kids or other dependents and need it). They have a few grand stashed away—just in case. It's imperative in this era of questionable employment, of more frequent natural disasters than ever before, of teenagers who (being teenagers) drive not as well as the rest of us, that you are prepared for nasty surprises.

17.
Your home is a piggy bank, not a cash cow.

For a few rich years at the beginning of this century, many Americans decided that their homes—which we should remember were appreciating like crazy at the time—were cash cows that produced money instead of milk. Folks used this source of funds to pay for college, vacations, new cars, and credit card consolidations. Until 2008. The housing bubble popped and home equity cratered. A lot of those people are still suffering, still sitting underwater, still owing more on their mortgages than their homes are worth. Many haven't been able to refinance into the cheapest mortgages in history as a result.

The lesson: Your home is not a cash cow. It is a piggy bank. In paying your mortgage every month, without fail, you build yourself a supplemental savings account. And when you choose to sell it, years down the road, that account will have serious value, even if the value of your property hasn't skyrocketed, even if it has done little more—as an investment—than keep pace with inflation. Keep your hands off that pig.

18.

You will spend more with credit than with debit and more with debit than with cash.

When you buy something using a credit card, you are not spending your own money. Even if you fully intend on paying the money back that same month, this truth has been absorbed by your psyche. And for that reason, spending the money using a credit card is not nearly as painful as spending cash. Bring the green stuff and leave the plastic at home.

19.
Carry Benjamins, not Jacksons.

By similar logic, spending big bills is more painful than spending smaller ones. Ditch the $20s you get from the ATM and get $100s from the teller. They'll stay in your wallet longer—and you'll get richer as a result.

20.

Count dollars like calories.

Research has shown that keeping a food diary—writing down what you put into your mouth, habitually and without fail—keeps even the most troubled dieters honest. The same is true of tracking your spending. Most people have absolutely no idea where their money goes—particularly their cash. Tracking, whether you do it using pencil and paper or a Web or smartphone application, works. I know because I've done it. I know others who've done it. It will transform your financial life.

21.
Save *for* something.

Try telling yourself to save some extra money each month. Now try telling yourself to save some extra money each month because you want to go on vacation, throw a great birthday bash, put in new kitchen counters, or _____ (fill in your own desire here). It's significantly easier when there's something you want at the other end. And note: It'll be easier still if you have a visual image of the goal. It's not unquantifiable "retirement," or even your amorphous "retirement house," it's the ski-in, ski-out condo with the hot tub right off the slopes in Stowe. Niiice.

22.

You can recover from any financial problem by saving more.

23.
Aim for progress, not perfection.

Life happens. If you let it stop you in your tracks, you are never going to meet your financial goals. When life gets in your way, do what I do: Take a deep breath. Tweak your process a little bit so you'll succeed the next time. Then move on. Because here's what happens if, over the years, you miss saving the $100 I talked about in rule #13 on a few occasions maybe even a few dozen occasions? You'll end up with $400,000 instead of $435,557. That is still a lot of money. But if you quit the first time you miss saving the $100, you'll end up with much, much less.

24.
Saving is more important than investing.

Next time you stress about the stock market, remember this: The amount of money you manage to sock away is much more important than the return on that money. You can take my word for it. Or you can consider this eye-opening example: You save $250 a month, which you then invest. If you earn 6 percent on that money, a year from now you'll have $3,267. If you earn 10 percent, you'll have $3,311—$44 more. But what if you waited a month to start saving? Then, even at 10 percent you'd have $3,052—$215 less. What if you saved $200 a month instead of $250? Then, again at 10 percent, you'd have $2,649—$618 less. As your nest-egg grows and gets into the six figure range, the return on investment starts to matter more. But you can't get to that level if you don't start to save now. Right now.

25.

Doing nothing can be very expensive.

You put off buying a gift for your mother's birthday. It's a week away. Then it's tomorrow. When you finally pick something up, you don't have time to shop around for the best price and you have to shell out for overnight mail. Or you delay signing up for the retirement plan at work when the open enrollment period comes around. By the time your employer nudges you again, another year of not saving has gone by. Or you know you need to name guardians for your kids, but you put it off because you don't want to have to choose one of your siblings over another. Then something terrible happens.

When you choose not to act, you have still made a choice. And most of the time, the choice is a bad one.

PART 3

Avoid (Most) Debt

Some financial experts believe that all debt is bad; some even call it evil.

I am not one of them.

Without debt, I would never have been able to buy a house or a car.

I know many people who would never have been able to afford college.

In my book (pun intended), debt is a financial resource that you need to learn how to use—wisely.

Follow these rules and even a credit card becomes a useful weapon in your financial arsenal.

26.

Just because someone will lend it to you doesn't mean you should borrow it.

This is the lesson of every unfurnished McMansion from Maine to California.

27.
Good debt is usually cheaper.

Good debt is debt that gets you something important—the roof over your head, the car you drive back and forth to work, a college education. You can often discern it from bad debt not just because bad debt is incurred for things you don't really need (and sometimes don't even really want) but because the interest rate will often be both lower and, in the case of a mortgage, tax deductible.

28.
Even good debt isn't free.

A debt's real cost is in opportunities lost. When you take on a new monthly payment (even one at a low interest rate), you're making a commitment against your future income—often for a very long period of time. What could you have done with the $423 a month you spent on the second car? Over a month, not much. But over 60 months, that's more than $20,000. Committing to debt prevents you from taking advantage of other opportunities that may come your way. You want to take a lower paying job because you love it? That's tough to do with a new second car sitting in the driveway.

29.
Use your emergency savings for emergencies.

The refrigerator goes kaput. The plumbing in the basement springs a leak. You need a pricey medical test that isn't covered by insurance. These are emergencies. Which is why I'm always amazed that people with emergency cushions panic and put these expenses on their credit cards. Use the cushion. Replenish it when you're out of the woods.

30.
Every birthday, check your weight and your credit score.

One should go down, the other should go up. Guess which? (Granted, both should stay level if they're already good.) It's important to understand how vital your credit score has become. It is now considered an important barometer of how responsible a human being you are. It will be used to decide: Do you get the car loan or the apartment or the job? Do you pay a decent rate for homeowner's insurance or credit card, or do you pay up? For those reasons, it's imperative to protect your score by doing all the things that positively affect it: Pay your bills on time; don't use more than 10 to 30 percent of your available credit; don't apply for new cards willy nilly; and don't cancel cards you're not using. The longer your open accounts are in good standing, the better your score.

Also remember: Looking at your report and finding items that look unfamiliar could mean identity theft. Check one report from each of the three credit bureaus for free each year at annualcreditreport.com.

31.
Don't borrow more for college than you expect to earn the first year out of school.

Parents listen up: Your kids may be irrational about this. They may have dreams of being the journalist or computer programmer or paralegal who sets new records for entry-level salaries. Don't allow your kids to borrow more for college than they expect they will earn in the first year out of school. I know (as the parent of two teens) that requires asking 17- and 18-year-olds what they might do when they graduate college, which is a pretty impossible question for most to answer. But it argues for being conservative in the amount of debt you—and they— take on. Even lawyers aren't earning what they used to.

32.
Your retirement trumps their tuition.

You know when you're on an airplane and they always tell you to put your oxygen mask on first before assisting a child? Saving for long-term financial needs is the same. If you don't save for your own future first, you won't be able to help your children when they need it. Worse, they may be forced to help you just when they're trying to put their own kids through school. There is no financial aid for retirement. There is plenty of financial aid for college. Don't feel guilty about this.

33.

The Joneses are in debt.

Remember this: If you look at the averages, chances are those people down the block (you know, the ones you envy) probably aren't doing as well as you think. In the U.S. alone an estimated 115 million people have credit card debt. Of them, the average household is carrying $15,799. And a study published by the National Bureau of Economic Research this year found that about half of Americans would be unable to come up with $2,000 if they needed it in an emergency, meaning they have no cash cushion or savings to get them through a bind. In other words, there's a good chance your flashy next door neighbors have some flashy debt to match. Bottom line: Unless you've taken a look at the books, don't assume to know anyone's financial situation except your own. Make your life-style and purchasing decisions based on what you can afford, not what your peers are buying, and instead of coveting thy neighbor's car, try to feel smug about your fat retirement account, your zero credit card balances, and the car you own free and clear.

PART 4

Spend Wisely

It's not always easy to spend less than you make, but it can be done.

Adhere to the following set of rules and watch it happen.

These rules are designed to keep you from overspending on things you need.

They'll also keep you from spending at all on stuff you don't need, don't want all that much, but would buy anyway if you had the chance. . . .

34.
The best cost-cutting tool is a good night's sleep.

With the possible exception of prescription medication, flashlight batteries, bottled water (under the pressure of a hurricane), and a few other true necessities, there is nothing you need to buy that can't wait until tomorrow. So when you're faced with a discretionary purchase, do your wallet a favor and sleep on it. If you're not still thinking about it—whatever it happened to be— 24 hours later, you didn't need or want it anyway.

35.

Just because you have a coupon doesn't mean you should go shopping.

36.

It is easy to buy things. It's hard to sell things. And it's even harder to sell things at a profit.

This is true of real estate. Stocks. Art. Jewelry. Technology. Cars. In fact, if you can come up with examples where this isn't true, I want to know about them.

37.
Free can be expensive.

My father always said there's no free lunch. He was right. There is a cost to everything and if you can't measure the cost in dollars, you have to measure it in time. That "free" phone you get for signing up for wireless service? It requires a long-term contract. The free companion airline ticket? You have to buy the first one at full price. Even free directory assistance requires you to listen to annoying advertisements before you get your listing. It's not that you shouldn't take advantage of these offers. But you should understand what you're really paying.

38.
Pay bills as they come in.

This is not as much about saving you money as it is about saving your sanity. People who pay their bills as they come in are happier. Why? Because if you get, say, a heating bill that's larger than you anticipated and you deal with it immediately, you'll make compromises on your other spending through the rest of the month so you come out whole. Also, sitting down at a table (or computer) and paying a stack of bills is mentally draining; watching that money fly out of your account and into someone else's is even worse.

39.

Always get three bids. Never take the high one.

40.

If it's good for the planet, it's usually good for your wallet.

Think: small cars, programmable thermostats, compact fluorescent lightbulbs, a garden, refilling your own water bottle . . . the list goes on.

41.
When it's 50% off, it's still 50% on.

There's a four-letter word that can light up your brain like few others: S-A-L-E. In particular, you're likely to be susceptible when there's a big price gap between the original price and the discount, when there's an offer on the table for a limited time only, and when you're not paying with real money (but with a credit card). Closing one of these transactions feels like a trophy. It feels like you've won. The problem is, although there are times that's true, there are others when the deal leads you to fork over money for things you neither really want nor really need. You lose.

42.
Don't shop angry.

Remember the scene from *Groundhog Day* when Bill Murray, loopy from waking up in Punxatawney for what was likely the 300th day, actually put the groundhog behind the wheel. "Don't drive angry," he cautioned. Well, you shouldn't shop—or invest—angry either. That's because anger makes you more optimistic and more of a risk taker than you'd naturally be. That means you're more likely to say "what the hell" to unfortunate purchases, to spend or invest money on a whim. Bad move. Similarly . . .

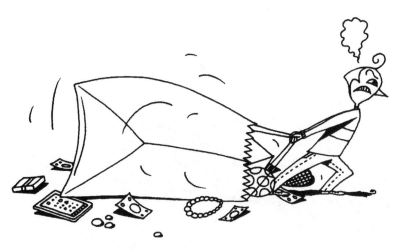

43.
Don't shop sad.

Feeling sad—because your team just lost the big game or you just suffered a disappointment at work—makes you eager to buy just about anything, research shows. Sadness feels like a big hole or void and you want to fill it up so you'll do whatever it takes and if you happen to have a credit card in your hand, so be it. And . . .

44.
Don't shop hungry.

This is not just a rule that applies in grocery stores. Do you know why they ply you with samples at warehouse stores? Because exciting your mouth—literally making you drool—makes you spend more money not just on food, but on everything. It primes the same part of your brain that responds to the rewards you really want. So maybe you went to the store to buy diapers but now that your brain is active, you buy the tent. (That shopping trip is legend in our family. I should tell you: We don't camp.) Oh, and when your favorite little boutique offers a special evening sale with wine and cheese? Steer clear. Alcohol not only primes the pleasure pump, it inhibits self-control.

45.

Shop with cheapskates.

Our friends influence everything from how much we eat to how much we spend. It's only human: Your best friend ordering dessert gives you license to do the same. And watching others swipe their credit cards makes you want to swipe yours, too. If you're trying to stick to a budget, and you need to go to the mall to grab a birthday present or a new pair of running shoes, pick your frugal friend, the one who clips coupons and runs her own running shoes into the ground—quite literally—over the one who shows up at every girls' night out twirling a new handbag.

46.
The salesperson is not your friend.

We shop for many reasons—including loneliness. This is important to remember when you stop at the mall on your way home from work because your spouse is working late, the kids have their own lives, and you just don't want to make dinner for one. You don't need anything in particular. What you're really craving is human contact. Those salespeople who tell you how great that leather jacket looks or what a deal you're getting on those towels aren't just being nice. They're doing their jobs and their jobs are to get you to open your wallet. You get caught up in the experience, the compliments, the camaraderie. They get commissions.

47.
Shop with a list.

Last year more than 80 percent of Americans made impulse purchases. Many spent hundreds, if not thousands, without planning on it. That's rent. Or a car payment. The best way to avoid this is to write down what you need. And unless you see it in black and white, don't buy it.

48.

If you're "just looking," don't try it on.

You're in the department store or your favorite boutique and you see a pair of pants that looks interesting. Unless you're in that store to buy pants, don't try them on. Why? Because behavioral economists have found that when you put those pants on and see yourself in them, your mind actually takes possession of them. At that point, not buying the pants feels like a loss. And as you'll see in rule #58, losing—particularly when it comes to money, but also when it comes to possessions—is particularly painful, and humans will do just about anything to avoid it. So you end up buying those pants you can't afford. Don't start the cycle.

49.
Don't budget while you're dieting. Don't diet when you're budgeting.

You probably think of willpower as unlimited. It's not. Psychologists now talk about ego depletion, the finding that willpower can lapse, especially when you're trying too hard to control yourself. The lesson: Don't work on more than one thing at a time that requires great willpower. Instead, prioritize and take them in turn.

50.
Don't use an ATM in a place without an easy exit.

This isn't a safety rule, it's a savings rule. ATM fees tend to go sky high in places where machines are in short supply—and cash in great demand. Casinos. Airports. Cruise ships. They're also high in theme parks, but for another reason. When you've paid for the express purpose of having fun, going to the parking lot to get in your car and drive to a nearby bank becomes a hassle you really want to avoid. You'll often pay up as a result.

51.
In any transaction, ask, "What's in it for them"?

Whenever there's a person on the other side of the table, it's crucial to know how they benefit from your spending. Think about agents: real estate agents, insurance agents, and the like. Even the ones "working for you," have an incentive to get you to pay as much as possible. When you buy a house, the agents and/or brokers (yours and theirs) each get a percentage. When buying life insurance, how much of a commission does your agent stand to make each year you pay your premiums? This rule also extends to pretty much every negotiation. Whether you're selling something of value, angling for your next raise, or the buyer, figuring out what's in it for the person (or people) on the other side of the deal will help you get the best deal for yourself.

52.

A sale isn't worth the drive if it doesn't save you more than the cost of the gas to get there.

53.
It's not about having it all. It's about having what you value most.

Money is a limited resource—and that means you can't have everything. Spend your money in a way that you're satisfied, not remorseful, after you do it. One way to get there is to track not only where you spend your money, but how you feel about the purchases you make. You thought that carpet cleaner charged too much? The restaurant portion was too small? You retired that jacket after two wearings? Write your feelings down. You won't make the same mistake again.

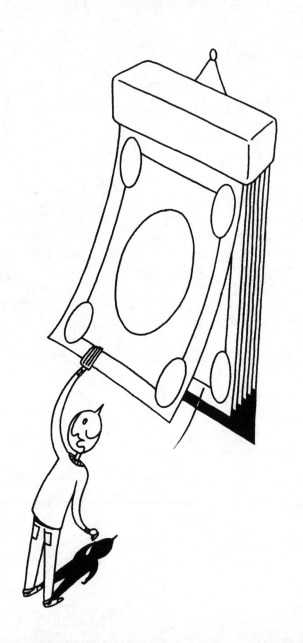

PART 5

Invest for Tomorrow

Once you've nailed the earnings strategies and savings strategies, you want to make sure that your money is working as hard for you as you are working for yourself.

Many financial professionals make this aspect of your life more complicated than it needs to be.

The rules in this section will help you filter out the important information from the sales pitch.

54.
Boring is better.

Individual stocks and managed mutual funds are exciting. Index funds and Exchange Traded Funds, or ETFs (which are funds that trade like stocks), are not. Why? With the latter type, a computer—not a Mercedes-driving fund manager—picks your investments. Index funds and ETFs strictly track a group of investments that all have something in common—the S&P 500 Index or Russell 2000 Index or Total Bond Market, for example. There's no sizzle. But these investments are cheaper to buy, cheaper to own, and cheaper on taxes. That's why over the long run they clean those actively-managed funds' clocks.

55.
The bottom line is the only line that matters.

How much was your car? How much was your house? Think twice before you answer with the sticker price. That $25,000 car didn't cost you $25,000. It likely cost another $1,500 in sales tax and another $3,000 or so in interest. Your house may cost you double the sticker by the time you're done paying it off. Investments work similarly. The average expenses on a stock mutual fund are around 1.3 to 1.5 percent. There are some that are significantly cheaper (0.25 percent) and others much more pricey (2 percent or more). Buy one of the cheaper ones and it means the fund that returns an average 8 percent per year is returning 7.75 percent; buy one of the more expensive ones and it takes that real return down to 6 percent. And just in case you're tempted to think that the higher fees are somehow worth it, they're generally not. The Security Exchange Commission (SEC) itself says "higher expense funds do not, on average, perform better than lower expense funds."

56.
Rebalance every
6 months . . .

Nine out of 10 investors don't rebalance—they don't
go through a regularly scheduled process of buying
or selling to keep up with movements in the market.
Many of them mean to. They want to. But they don't.
Sometimes, life gets in the way. Other times, their
portfolios are performing so well they can't stand
to take profits off the table. It's crucial. If you don't
rebalance, swings in the market can force you into a
position where you're taking too much or too little
risk. Neither of which is a good thing.

57.
... Or buy investments where you don't have to.

If you know you'll never rebalance, buy an investment that will rebalance itself. I'm talking about a target-date retirement fund, an all-in-one investment that is managed according to your retirement date. (The age-based portfolios in some 529 college savings plans work this way too.) These investments take more risk when you have decades until retirement and less when you get closer. In a down market they won't prevent you from losing money, but research shows, they will prevent you from losing as much as you would have otherwise.

58.
Losing money hurts more than it should.

Your brain dreads losing money twice as much as it enjoys making it. That's why investors tend to hold tanking stocks far too long, rather than cut their losses. It's also why some investors don't rebalance—which requires you to sell some winning investments (eliminating the chance of further profits) and load up on others that aren't doing so well. If you see yourself in these descriptions, take the control out of your own hands using rules #56 and #57.

59.

Nobody cares about your money as much as you do.

60.
Even money managers need managing.

Bernard Madoff scared the world when it was revealed he wasn't actually investing the billions of dollars entrusted to his care, but rather using the money to fund his long-running Ponzi scheme. Of course, that's extreme. But unless you keep an eye on your money manager, you may easily end up taking on too much risk, paying unnecessary fees or expenses or owning investments you don't know about or understand. You'll know you're doing your job if you can answer the following two questions: How much is this relationship costing me? And is it worth it? And the answer to the second one is "yes."

61.
Diversify

No one knows for sure where the markets are going. That makes being an investor frightening. But one thing we do know for sure is that different segments of the markets—stocks and bonds, for example—tend to do well at different times. So, owning bonds is a form of insurance against owning stocks and vice versa. And having both tends to mean that although you won't do as well as if you'd only held the winning assets (which, again, you cannot predict) by holding both you don't lose your shirt. Holding these different asset classes—not just stocks and bonds, but cash, real estate, and precious metals—as well as subclasses of all of these assets—domestic and international and emerging markets, large and small, etc.—is called diversification. It sounds complicated but it's actually very easy to diversify. You do it when you buy target-date funds (rule #57) but you can also do it by purchasing total stock market or total bond market funds. Then you own just about everything. When investors talk about not putting all of their eggs in one basket, this is what they mean. And it's more important than it has ever been before.

62.
Automate.

As I mentioned in the introduction to this book, you have a 50 percent chance of running out of money in retirement. Cut your odds: Automate your investment contributions and increase your percentages with every pay raise. If you've never saved before and money's tight, start with 3 percent of your pay—if money's not tight, start higher—then increase your contribution 2 percent a year until you max out. The goal is to be socking away 10 percent a year if you start before your mid thirties (that can include matching contributions from your employer) and 15 percent a year if you start later than that. And note: Just participating in a work-based retirement plan slims the chance of running out of money to 20 percent. That's huge.

63.

If you can't explain it, don't buy it.

64.

If you can't figure out what an investment (or financial advisor) is costing you, you're overpaying.

65.
If there's already a bandwagon, you're too late to get on it.

Think back to the dot-com boom. If you were fortunate enough to hear about Amazon or eBay before all your friends, and you quietly did a little research and bought some shares, more power to you. By the time that these companies—or any investments—are the latest cocktail party conversation or newspaper headline, it's too late.

66.
Ask: "What's the worst that could happen"?

Always ask that question—and know the answer—before you invest in anything. Could you lose it all? Could you be stuck not being able to get your money back if and when you need it? Or is the worst case that your money will sit there and earn you nothing—which means you're losing after taxes and inflation. Understanding the upside is only half of what you need to know before making any important investment decisions.

67.
Bad news is often followed by worse news.

If a company you're holding announces bad news, ask yourself: Is this a one-time blip? Or is this the first in a series of similar announcements? That's what happened with Enron. With Worldcom. With Lucent. Many people hold on to these sinking ship stocks too long because they're either too paralyzed or too optimistic to make a move. This is particularly true if you happen to work for the company at hand. Don't get sucked in. Where there is smoke, there may be fire.

68.

He who panics first, panics best.

By the same token, as the whispers turn sour on any investment (not gossipy whispers but the sort that indicate something is deeply, fundamentally wrong—the market for the product is drying up, the company just lost a major patent challenge, the CEO is being investigated by the SEC) sell first and ask questions later.

69. Date your stocks, don't marry them.

You're likely to have an abundance of confidence in any investment you take the time to research and choose yourself. This makes you feel as if you're in control of what happens to the investment—which of course you never are. If any of these self-selected investments dives 10 percent, out of sync with the market as a whole, take a hard look at what's going in that business and don't let any psychological attachment get in the way of cold analysis.

70.
Keep your hands off your retirement funds. Period.

If you pull money out of your 401(k), IRA, or other retirement accounts before you hit age 59½, you'll have to pay income taxes as well as a 10 percent penalty. That can cost 30-plus cents on the dollar. Any money you remove also loses its ability to grow tax-deferred until you retire. If you switch jobs, leave the money in the current plan, transfer it to your new employer's plan, or roll it into an IRA to maintain its tax-advantaged status.

71.

The market doesn't make mistakes. People do.

72.
The secret to successful investing isn't talent or timing. It's temperament.

Do you have it in you to ignore the short-term volatility in the markets? To keep buying when the picture looks dimmest? And to acknowledge that you do not know where the markets are going day to day, week to week, or even month to month? Then you have what it takes to be a good investor. It's sad, but true: Human psychology works against the behaviors that have historically led to good long-term returns. If you can acknowledge this truth and work within it—raising the white flag and getting some help when you feel yourself wavering—you'll be just fine.

73.

Hope is not an investment strategy.

74.
"Be fearful when others are greedy and be greedy when others are fearful."

Warren Buffett said that. And you should consider putting that advice into practice. Big rapid sell-offs in the market—think the oil shocks, the crash of 1987, the savings and loan crisis, the long-term capital management debacle, the tech crisis, and the 2008 downturn—present an opportunity for investors who have cash on the sidelines. You can get in, buy some specific stocks you always wanted (or the market as a whole), and reap the upside.

75.
Don't drink *all* the Kool-Aid.

As an employee, chances are you believe in what your company is doing. That means if the business falls on hard times, you may be unwilling or unable to believe it. (See rule #67.) That's why you should never keep more than 10 percent of your money in your company's stock. Moreover, if your firm does take a turn for the worse, not only will you feel it in your portfolio, you may lose your job. That sort of doubling down never makes sense.

76.

Big numbers make smart people do stupid things.

Think of Sarah Ferguson, caught on tape attempting to sell access to her ex-husband for a half million pounds. Or think of lottery tickets. When the jackpot is a regular size, people buy a regular number of tickets. Or they don't buy at all. But once the Powerball jackpot gets into the hundreds of millions, we go nuts to get our hands on tickets—even though the chances of winning have actually gone way, way down. The same happens with the sort of hot tips—and big projections—you see as investors. The big numbers make you even more eager to buy in. What you should be instead is more disciplined and discerning.

77.
No one really knows where the market is going.

People who say they do are advertising the fact that at one time or another they just got lucky.

PART 6

Cover Your Assets

Once you begin to amass savings, investments, real estate, and other possessions, you need a plan in place to protect those assets.

Even more important, once you start a family, the people in that family need protecting as well.

You cover your assets in two ways—by purchasing insurance and creating an estate plan that establishes some ground rules about how your assets would be handled if you weren't able to do it yourself. None of these things are easy.

They force you to think about things you'd rather not think about.

They also make you spend money that—in the best possible circumstances—you're essentially throwing down the drain. That's why this next set of rules is, perhaps, the most important of all.

78.

The biggest threat to your financial security is your health.

Medical debt is the leading cause of personal bankruptcy in the U.S. Think about the last person you know who was laid low by cancer or leveled by a heart attack. Not too hard to come up with an example, is it? And every year, you'll know more and more victims. This is why you must buy health insurance, even if all you can afford is a high-deductible policy that covers only worst-case scenarios.

79.
If you can't afford to replace it, insure it. If you can afford to replace it, don't.

This rule applies for pretty much all kinds of insurance. Replacing your brand new car would be a hardship, so you insure it; replacing your old clunker wouldn't, so you drop the collision coverage. Replacing a $10,000 engagement ring would require you to save for months, so you buy a separate policy (called a rider). Having to replace a $500 ring might bum you out—but it wouldn't mean you couldn't pay the mortgage. No rider in this case (your homeowner's policy will likely pick up the tab). You'll make the right decision on life insurance if you think about it as income insurance. If there are people who need your income and wouldn't be able to replace it without you—buy it. If you don't have these sorts of dependents (spouses, kids, older parents), don't.

80.
Life insurance is (usually) a lousy investment.

Most people are better off buying term life insurance than buying permanent insurance. Term life is a death benefit, pure and simple. And it's much, much cheaper. Permanent insurance—whole life or universal life—combines that death benefit with an investment component and is much more complicated and expensive. Term is best for most people. Because by the time you hit retirement and your term policy "terminates," the idea is that the mortgage will be largely paid off, college will be done, and the kids will be off the dole, at which point the needs of your dependents are much less. You won't need the life insurance anymore because if one of you were to die, you could support the other with your existing assets alone. If that's not how you see your life unfolding and you believe—because you have a special needs child or you want to use insurance to leave an inheritance— that you want life insurance in place forever, then it makes sense to look at permanent life insurance. But as insurance, not as an investment.

81.
The harder the sell, the faster you should run.

Do you need that insurance at the rental car counter? Not if your own policy—or your credit card—already provides it. And that's not the only example. Think of the extended warranties they sell at the big box stores. Or the mortgage life insurance you're offered shortly after you signed on the dotted line to buy a home. The harder the sell, the greater the chances that you don't need it. At all.

82.

Quit smoking: Cigarettes cost $150 a pack.

The cigarettes themselves are just a tiny part of that the total price per pack. You've got life insurance rates that are four times higher and corporations charging higher health insurance premiums to their employees who smoke. You'll pay more for auto insurance and homeowner's insurance—and when you go to sell your home or car you'll get a lower price because the smell can cause the value to go down. And then there's the decreased value of your lifetime earnings. The list goes on, but the point is clear: Nipping your habit is not just a good health decision. It's a smart financial one.

83.
Lose weight: Being overweight costs you $524 a year if you're a woman and $432 if you're a man.

Being obese costs six to nine times that much. As with smokers, overweight people pay more for life insurance. Out-of-pocket medical costs run substantially higher and salaries (especially in women) are much, much lower. There are productivity costs, the costs of missing days at work, even added fuel costs because it costs more to run your car. So, if you were looking for motivation . . . here it is in black and white. And remember, studies have shown if you make progress in one area of your life, other improvements tend to follow.

84.
Banking online makes you smarter and safer.

Sure it saves you time (roughly 2 hours a month) and money (about $60 bucks a year in stamps) but that's not why you should do it. Research has shown people who bank online look at their accounts four times more often than people who bank the old-fashioned way. And just looking at your money is a great way to notice if something fishy is going on in your accounts. That means if you happen to be one of the nearly 10 million annual victims of identity theft, you'll notice it—and be able to shut it down—sooner.

85.

Six words to close any deal: "Can I get that in writing"?

This rule exists not just so that if you have a problem obtaining the service at hand you'll have a contract you can use to force the other party to make it right. Defending contracts often costs more money than they're worth. Rather, getting it in writing has another purpose: Clarity. When you get it in writing, you have a basis for comparison. You can compare different estimates or proposals to see which one lines up with your needs and your budget. You also have a true, line-by-line sense of just what you've signed up for, when it will be delivered, and how much it's going to cost you. In other words, you have back-up.

86.

Shred.

If it has your social security number, account number, password, PIN, or signature on it, shred it. If it has your phone number, birth date, e-mail address, name, or address on it, consider shredding it. All of that information can be used to steal your identity. Even in this high-tech age, dumpster divers still routinely go through trash bins to pull snippets of paper they can use to swipe checking account balances, load up your credit cards with fraudulent charges, or worse. Don't give them the chance.

87.
Your heart will stop or the tumor will grow.

No one likes to think about this, but you must put your life in order for the people who love you. Four documents will do the trick: A *will* determines who gets your stuff and, if applicable, custody of your kids. A *living will* tells a hospital whether you want life support. A *healthcare proxy* lets someone else make medical decisions for you if you can't do it for yourself, and a *durable power of attorney* does the same for your finances. Depending on how complicated (and rich) your financial life is, you may also want a trust or two that further stipulate how your assets pass to your heirs and can help you avoid estate taxes. But the aforementioned four are the biggies. If you've got them, you've done your job.

88.

Spend more time building a legacy than an inheritance.

What's more valuable: leaving $20,000 to you kids, or instilling a work ethic that lets them earn an extra $20,000 a year?

PART 7

Do's and Don'ts

There are some rules that don't fall into any of the aforementioned categories—yet they are rules nonetheless.

They might save your friendships.

They might improve your marriage.

They will certainly preserve your sanity.

Ignore them at your peril.

89.
Don't lend money to friends and relatives.

If you have it to spare—and you (a) feel the urge and (b) are pretty sure you won't resent it—give it away. But becoming the bank makes them feel guilty and you parental. You'll never be able to go out to dinner again without thinking: "He ordered steak?" or "Those look like new shoes." If you can't afford it, or will resent it, offer to help with information, just not cold hard cash.

90.
Don't co-sign.

The FTC estimates that as many as three out of four co-signers end up repaying defaulted loans. Of course, co-signing sometimes seems unavoidable. The person asking you to do it is, undoubtedly, someone you're close to and someone you trust. It can be difficult to understand why the big bad lender can't see in this person all that you do. Trust me, they have a reason. That person's credit score isn't high enough; they don't have enough of a credit history to qualify for the loan on their own; or the lender has deemed they can't afford the monthly payments. All three are reason to walk away. If you don't, you'll likely be sorry.

91.

Don't take financial advice from someone just because they're wealthy (or related).

92.
Don't hire 'em if you can't look 'em in the eye.

If you can't be as open and honest with a financial advisor or lawyer as you would to, say, your gynecologist (guys, insert your own example here), you won't give that person all of the information needed to create the right plan for you. As a result, you won't get a plan that fits your needs and objectives. The person on the other side of the table may be a fine advisor, but if you don't feel comfortable around them, he or she is not the advisor for you.

93.
Do declare some financial independence.

Just because you marry someone (or love them enough to live with them) doesn't make you the same person. You need some money of your own so that you can make small financial decisions—like whether to eat lunch out, whether to purchase that tie— without asking permission. Without it, financial relationships start to feel parental rather than romantic. Having some money—particularly invest-ments—of your own also forces you into the position of having to manage it. That's not a bad thing either. How much "me" money should you have? Figure out what's left after you've paid the monthly bills and saved 10 percent (or more). You can divvy up the rest.

94.
Do give back.

People who spend money and time on charity are healthier and happier. They sleep more and exercise more and that puts them in a better frame of mind. Giving back—doing something for someone else, whether you write a check, volunteer, or give away your unwanted things—gives the human psyche a boost that's hard to replicate in any other way. And I truly believe that practicing gratitude is also the antidote to materialism. Think about it: Materialism is focusing on what you want, obsessing on what you desire. Gratitude is being thankful for what you already have.

The Last Word

Finally, try to remember that in most cases, money doesn't cause your problems. You may have a work problem, an idea problem, a motivation problem, an organization problem, or a relationship problem. You don't have a money problem. But lack of money is the result. Focus on understanding and then unwinding the underlying issue—even if you didn't do anything wrong to cause it. (Homeowners underwater because they purchased a fairly-valued house in 2006 come to mind.) Then use the rules—and the guiding principles—to help you find your way.

If you have a favorite Money Rule, I'd love to see it. Please send it to me at facebook.com/jeanchatzky or @jeanchatzky on Twitter. Thanks!

Acknowledgments

As I explained in the introduction, these are not just my Money Rules. They were gathered from many generous sources who were happy to be able to spread the wealth, so to speak, and for that I am grateful to: Nathan Bachrach, Erin Baehr, Tracy Beard, Randy Beeman, Colin Carter, Steve Cassaday, Roger Coleman, Lee DeLorenzo, Edgar Dworsky, Steve Ely, Gregg Fisher, Stacey Francis, Meg Green, Keith Gumbinger, Kathleen Gurney, Joel Issacson, Hugh Johnson, Mark Kantrowitz, Ben Kaplan, Eliot Kaplan, Susan Kaplan, Rick Kahler, Jean Keener, Michael Klein, Steve Lockshin, Tim Maurer (who gets a shout-out for pointing out that personal finance is more personal than finance), Greg Miller, Tom Posey, Gary Ran, Carl Richards, Rebecca Rothstein, Gretchen Rubin, David Rubinger, Richard Saperstein, Gary Schatsky, Barry Schwartz, Paul Tramontano, John Waldron, Jeff Yeager, and David Zier.

A big thank-you to Arielle O'Shea and Maggie McGrath. Both did excellent reporting for this project (and contributed some Money Rules of their own).

It has been a pleasure for me to have the opportunity to work with the team at Rodale: David Zinczenko, Steve Perrine, Mike Zimmerman, Diane Salvatore, Margot Gilman, Michele Promaulayko, George Karabotsos, Mark Michaelson, and Marilyn Hauptly. I want to thank all of you for getting behind this project.

Finally, there are those people—professional and personal—who always have my back. To borrow a song title from Kelly Clarkson, who I suspect knows all the rules, my life would suck without . . . Richard Pine, Richard Leibner, Jamie Brickell, Jeffrey Johnson, Laurie Hosie, Ashley Sandberg, John Ferriter, George Arquilla, Michael Falcon, Melisa Schilling, Jim Bell, Matt Lauer, Ann Curry, Al Roker, Natalie Morales, Savannah Guthrie, Hoda Kotb, Kathie Lee Gifford, Jackie Levin, Marc Victor, Debbie Kosovsky, Noah Kotch, the Money 911 team (Alicia Ybarbo, Gil Reisfield, Donna Nichols, Amanda Avery, Liz Neumann), Beth O'Connell, Frances Severance, Diane Adler, Jan Fisher, Jodie Smoler, Roberta Socolof, Kathy Goldberg, Debi Fried, Laura Mogil, Hillary Messer, Claudia Grassey, Denise Rubin Carter, Ilene Miller, and Gary Greenwald.

And to my family—Eliot, Jake, Julia, Sam, Emily, Dave, Ali, Eric, Elaine and Bob—maybe the things you can't fix with duct tape can be tackled by the rules herein.